Original title:
Interstellar Haikus

Copyright © 2025 Creative Arts Management OÜ
All rights reserved.

Author: Maxwell Donovan
ISBN HARDBACK: 978-1-80567-777-2
ISBN PAPERBACK: 978-1-80567-898-4

Twilight Among the Stars

The sky spills some juice,
Starlight giggles and swirls,
Planets play hide and seek,
Comets dance with a twirl.

Aliens sip their tea,
Asteroids roll on by,
Nebulae throw a party,
Black holes just can't lie.

Celestial Footsteps

Moonwalkers in a daze,
Tripping on space dust trails,
Shooting stars are just darts,
Venus yells, 'No fails!'

Saturn wears a bowtie,
Jupiter plays charades,
Mars takes all the selfies,
With laughs that won't fade.

The Language of the Universe

Stars whisper in Morse code,
Planets giggle back loud,
Galaxies form a band,
Singing to the crowd.

A comet cracks a joke,
Black holes laugh till they choke,
Supernovae snicker,
As they burst into smoke.

Resonance of the Void

In the void, murmurings,
Echoes bounce like a ball,
Cosmic hiccups abound,
Quasars having a ball.

In this silly ballet,
Where gravity likes to play,
The universe chuckles,
Through night into day.

The Shimmering Abyss

In the deep abyss,
A fish wears a space suit,
Sipping cosmic tea,
And chatting with a moon.

Galloping comets,
Laughing in zero g,
Taco-shaped asteroids,
Dance around the stars.

A black hole giggles,
Pulling socks, not ships,
What a cosmic prank,
Gravity's silly joke.

Floating through stardust,
Wormholes look like smiles,
In this vast wonder,
The universe chuckles.

Spheres of Resplendent Light

Planets in a line,
Wearing silly hats now,
Orbiting the sun,
While the stars roll their eyes.

Jellybean-shaped moons,
Playing hide and seek there,
Laughing meteorites,
Throwing space confetti.

Galaxies unite,
In a dance-off at night,
Cosmic disco balls,
Shimmering with delight.

Spheres of bright chaos,
Bouncing all around free,
What a cosmic joke,
In this wild galaxy.

Shadows of Forgotten Realms

Shadows whisper tales,
Of socks lost in the void,
Echos laugh softly,
As galaxies snooze on.

Forgotten realms twirl,
With dust bunnies in flight,
Vast and endless dreams,
In dark matter's embrace.

A nebula sneezes,
Spreading colors like paint,
It tickles a comet,
Drawing laughter from stars.

In shadows they laugh,
At the cosmic mishaps,
Where giggles echo,
In infinite dark spaces.

The Language of Starlight

Stars giggle and wink,
In a tongue made of light,
Whispering jokes bright,
Through the velvet of night.

Planets share secrets,
In circles of bright glow,
A comet's quick dash,
Is the ultimate show.

The sun can't keep still,
With its rays full of fun,
Joking with the moons,
While they play in the sun.

Language of starlight,
Speaks in giggles and beams,
Cosmic humor flows,
In the galaxy's dreams.

Celestial Dust Bunnies

In the cosmic sweep,
Bunnies float all around,
Hiding in stardust,
Chasing comets down.

Lunar hopscotch games,
Their tails twitch with delight,
Playing tag with planets,
Underneath the moonlight.

They bounce on starlit waves,
Crumbs of space cookies fly,
Sipping on starlight gin,
And giggling in the sky.

When shooting stars go by,
They giggle and they squeal,
With every flash of light,
Their joy is truly real.

Between Twilight and Dawn

Fluffy clouds take flight,
On wings of coffee dreams,
Between dark and light,
They dance in silent beams.

Jupiter's bright grin,
Sips tea with Saturn's rings,
They gossip of the night,
And all its strange things.

Stars play hide and seek,
In the cloak of the dark,
Whispers of giggles,
Paint the universe' spark.

As dawn tips its hat,
The heavens crack a smile,
Another day begins,
Twilight's charm; it's worth the while.

Visions Beyond the Veil

Aliens send memes,
From galaxies alive,
Their humor so bizarre,
It makes the cosmos thrive.

With Cosmic TikTok dances,
They flaunt their weird moves,
Floating in the vacuum,
They've got all the grooves.

Through portals and portholes,
Jokes blink in and out,
Why did Pluto cross?
To show he's still about!

Bellies full of laughter,
They burst like supernovae,
In the vast unknown,
There's fun to find every day.

Gravitational Lullabies

Moonbeams gently hum,
To comets on their way,
Their lullabies entice,
Stars to play and sway.

Singing to the void,
With a twinkle and a wink,
Asteroids join in too,
And start to dance and clink.

Galaxies in pajamas,
Doze softly on a cloud,
Twirling in their dreams,
While the universe is loud.

As they drift toward sleep,
Cosmic giggles resound,
In the cradle of space,
Joy and wonder abound.

Distant Luminary Auras

Stars are quite gassy,
But they twinkle with flair.
Pull on those big breezes,
Shining everywhere!

Suns are just big bulbs,
Lighting up the night sky,
Some might feel lonely,
But they never cry!

Galaxy swings wildly,
Like a cosmic dance craze.
Planets miss the beat,
In a dizzying haze.

Harmony of the Spheres

Asteroids are drummers,
Beating cosmic tunes.
Comets are the flutes,
With their icy runes.

Venus hums a song,
While Mars plays the bass,
Neptune's in the back,
Playing hide-and-chase.

Space is quite the racket,
With gravitational booms.
But in this great chaos,
We still sweep with brooms!

Echoing Through the Cosmos

Black holes like to gossip,
Spinning tales so wide.
Whispers of the universe,
In a swirling ride.

Light-years as our gossip,
Traveling so far.
News from the Milky Way,
You won't need a car!

Astro-birds chirp loudly,
Shooting stars take flight.
Cosmic banter echoes,
Through the endless night!

Orbit of Dreams

Sleeping in the stars,
Dreams touch every face.
Lunar lullabies,
In this wide embrace.

Planets toss and turn,
In their cloud-like beds.
Saturn spins in circles,
While Jupiter dreads.

Comets chase the night,
With a bright, icy grin.
Dreaming of their past,
When they all begin.

Planetary Rhythms

On Jupiter's dance,
Coffee beans do bounce.
Saturn's rings surprise,
With glitter and pounce.

Mars invites a laugh,
With dust storms that swirl.
Venus makes us blush,
In its hot, sultry pearl.

Comets try to race,
With tails so absurd.
Asteroids throw rocks,
Like toddlers stirred.

Neptune sings a tune,
In colors so bright.
Pluto just rolls eyes,
Claiming 'I'm still right!'

Galactic Reveries

Stars gossip at night,
In twinkling delight.
They trade funny tales,
Of comets in flight.

Black holes spin a yarn,
Of things that got lost.
Event horizon jokes,
Always at a cost.

Planets arm-wrestle,
Who's strongest of all?
Mars brags about strength,
Till gravity's call.

Aliens on lunch,
Share weird greenish stew.
They claim it's the best,
But who would chew?

Lightyears of Solitude

In vast empty space,
An echo of me.
My only friend here,
Is an old tin can, whee!

Years stretch for miles,
Lonely thoughts drift by.
Space can be a joke—
Or a funny bye-bye.

Martian memes are gold,
Sent in ones and twos.
"They caught me off guard,"
Says the alien snooze.

Time creates a jest,
As I float around.
The universe laughs,
While I wear a frown.

Cosmic Drift

Rockets make me cringe,
They tickle my fears.
But piñatas of stars,
Burst in cheers and tears.

Asteroids play catch,
In a game of space tag.
Saturn holds the prize,
A galactic swag bag.

Nebula-eye roll,
Clouds whisper and sway.
"Why don't you join us?
Just take a nice vacation, okay?"

Space-time folds a laugh,
In dimensions so wide.
Funny how we drift,
In this cosmic ride.

Celestial Echoes

In a starry night,
Aliens strolled in flight,
Waving at the moon,
Eating cosmic stew.

With space cats on leashes,
They hunt for lost treasures,
Juggling glowing asteroids,
And dancing with meteors.

Their laughter rings far,
A galaxy's bizarre.
Shooting stars take aim,
At space games they claim.

When gravity goes wild,
They flail like a child,
A wormhole trip planned,
But landed in quicksand.

Starlit Reflections

Under twinkling lights,
Space llamas take flights,
With helmets that shine,
In costumes divine.

They skateboard on rings,
With laughter that sings,
Eclipsing their foes,
In cosmic rodeos.

Chasing off comets,
Playing hopscotch on debts,
They trade stardust puns,
For intergalactic runs.

While planets all spin,
The laughter pours in,
With giggles and glee,
In this vast galaxy.

Nebulae's Secret Song

In colorful clouds,
The whispers are loud,
Singing tunes of joy,
To every girl and boy.

A cosmic karaoke,
With aliens quirky,
They croon 'til it glows,
While space-time just flows.

With balloons made of gas,
They float and they pass,
Gifting starlit smiles,
For luminous miles.

As quasars join in,
A funky spin win,
In a pink-hued whirl,
A funny space twirl.

Exoplanetary Glances

On strange worlds we roam,
With creatures from home,
They waddle and prance,
In a clumsy dance.

With three eyes, they blink,
And argue, then drink,
Galactic smoothie,
That tastes quite fruity.

They bet on the rise,
Of a new sun's surprise,
With popcorn in hand,
As a comet takes stand.

Back on Earth, they cheer,
With hoots we can hear,
As rockets take flight,
In this cosmic night.

Celestial Whispers

In space, cats float,
Chasing their tails in stars.
Planets are their toys,
Galaxies, their playgrounds.

Aliens giggle,
While sipping cosmic tea.
Asteroids dance jigs,
Comets wink and agree.

Martians play charades,
With echoes of laughter.
Black holes sigh in glee,
As they spin their own rafter.

Space cows moo in tune,
In the Milky Way's bar.
Venus loves a joke,
While Pluto's on guitar.

Nebula Dreams

Clouds of dust and gas,
Huddle in a soft bed.
Starry-eyed dreams spin,
While meteors hide dread.

Shooting stars race past,
On a cosmic bicycle.
Giggles in the night,
Make every journey cyclical.

Whimsical tron birds,
Chirp in astral delight.
They play tag with light,
In the velvet, deep night.

Nebulae burst forth,
In colors absurdly bright.
Chair-lifting pranks occur,
Gravities just can't fight.

Cosmic Threads

Weaving space and time,
With laughter as the loom.
Galactic yarns unwind,
Creating cosmic boom.

Planets knit in pairs,
With quirks beyond compare.
Saturn wears a hat,
Jupiter makes a glare.

Wormholes twist and twirl,
In a fashion show of stars.
Even black holes sport,
Brightly colored avatars.

Tangled in time's fab,
Asteroids join the spree.
With every cosmic stitch,
They giggle, wild and free.

Starlit Journeys

When rockets take flight,
Space snacks float everywhere.
Zero-gravity fun,
With popcorn in the air.

Stars sing silly songs,
On a rhythm of delight.
Alien DJ spins,
With a comet as the light.

Drifting through the void,
With clumsy, goofy grins.
Planetary disco,
Where everyone just spins.

Laughter lights the sky,
As they bounce from star to star.
Galactic giggle-fest,
Travels near and far.

Time Dilation

Wibbly wobbly time,
A clock strikes twice, oh dear!
Stop for a snack break,
Yet years just disappear.

Gravity's cruel prank,
Aging at a snail's pace,
My fingers are old,
With a youthful face.

Spaceship race on pause,
Laziness is the key,
While planets spin fast,
I enjoy my cup of tea.

Laughing through the stars,
As meteors fly past,
They wink and they smile,
Forever doomed to last.

Space's Solitary Breath

In the void, I sigh,
Echoes of cosmic snacks,
Cheese from other worlds,
Floating with no tracks.

My lonely space suit,
With a snack pocket too,
Galactic goldfish,
Tastes like outer stew.

Planets join the dance,
Gravity makes me trip,
I tumble through stardust,
On a cosmic flip.

Whispers in the dark,
Asteroids share some jokes,
With a touch of sass,
And a laugh that provokes.

Celestial Surfing

Riding solar waves,
On a comet's tail I glide,
Spaceboards made of light,
Come join the joyful ride!

Stardust in my hair,
Cosmic wipes across my face,
I wipe out again,
What a silly place!

Galaxies twirl past,
Like dancers in the night,
Spinning in circles,
Oh, what a delight!

Laughter fills the air,
As I catch a shooting star,
Falling into dreams,
Now I'm a space bar.

Galactic Serenade

Sing to the moonlight,
A symphony of stars,
Crickets on the Mars,
Play guitars from afar.

Neptune hums a tune,
As Jupiter taps his feet,
Cosmic karaoke,
Makes my evening sweet.

Asteroids beat drums,
In a jazzy parade,
While black holes mock me,
"Your rhythm's so delayed!"

Harmony in space,
A cosmic comedy,
Laughter with the stars,
Eternal jubilee!

Celestial Serenade

Stars are winking bright,
Why did Mars wear a tie?
Jupiter danced at night,
While Saturn just sighed, oh my!

Comets zoom around,
Grumpy moons play chess,
Galaxies spin 'round,
They all laugh, I guess!

Nebulas puff out jokes,
Black holes say, 'Whoa, wait!'
Space just loves its hoax,
Gravity can't take the bait!

In the cosmic lounge,
Aliens sip tea,
Time does a funny bounce,
They giggle, "Just be free!"

Quantum Murmurs

Photons giggle bright,
As they play peek-a-boo,
Quarks in silly fights,
'Are we here, or just two?'

Electrons spin around,
In a dance so bizarre,
One says, 'I've been found!'
The other shouts, 'No star!'

Waves crash like a joke,
Gravity joins the fun,
The universe bespoke,
'Why does matter run?'

Time trips on a dot,
Space teases with a wink,
It's a wild plot,
But who's got time to think?

Asteroid Chants

Asteroids in a race,
Rolling like a ball,
'Is this a serious place?'
They bicker and they brawl.

Hopping through the void,
One claims, 'I'm the best!'
Another, feeling annoyed,
Says, 'Let's just take a rest!'

Bouncing off each star,
They sing a silly tune,
'We're the champs, by far!'
Then get lost 'til noon.

Meteors that fall,
Tell tales of their fight,
While planets stand tall,
And laugh at their plight!

Stellar Reflections

In the light of stars,
Mirrors show their smiles,
Echoing from afar,
They share their cosmic styles.

A galaxy grins wide,
With cheeky little eyes,
It twirls and it glides,
While milky dustfly sighs.

Starlight beams a tease,
A twinkling little jest,
'Why can't we just freeze?'
'We're space's very best!'

The cosmos holds its breath,
In laughter's bright delight,
For amidst life and death,
Stars dance in the night!

Galaxies in Quietude

Stars giggle at night,
Planets play hide and seek,
A comet slips on ice,
Making space friends squeak.

Nebulae wear their wigs,
Dancing in cosmic cheer,
Aliens throw big parties,
Floating snacks, never fear.

Black holes munch on stardust,
Blooping sounds echo loud,
Starships trim their mustaches,
Daring, bold, and proud.

In this cosmic circus,
Laughter fills the voids bright,
Astronauts tell big tales,
In a dance of delight.

Ethereal Guardians

Little green creatures,
Swipe their phones on the moons,
Telling space dad jokes,
Shooting giggles and tunes.

Galactic butterflies,
Flutter with flair and swagger,
Spilling stardust giggles,
While constellations stagger.

Planetary pranks rule,
Asteroids juggling dreams,
Slapstick in zero G,
With galactic moonbeams.

Cosmic beings chuckle,
As they float and sway,
In this funny universe,
It's quite the cabaret!

Galaxies in Whisper

Tiny twinkling lights,
Whispering space secrets,
Traveller laughs aloud,
As gravity panics.

Meteors tailgate stars,
Making wishes go high,
Dusted off like old comments,
Then wave them goodbye.

Astro cats take moon baths,
Purring nebulae soft,
Chasing their tails through time,
As comets scoff and scoff.

Giggle at dark matter,
It's hiding, what a tease!
Cosmic fun forever,
In the cosmic breeze.

Cosmic Dreams Unfurled

Stars play jump rope here,
In a galaxy-wide game,
Asteroids yell 'tag!'
Oh, it's never the same!

Aliens share their snacks,
Fried comets and stardust,
Nibbling through the void,
In this cosmic gust.

Nebulae wear silly hats,
Floating through space with glee,
Guardians of the giggles,
In this fun jubilee.

As dreams drift in silence,
Cosmic laughter rings clear,
Join us in this frolic,
Space is full of cheer!

The Light of Farewell

Stars shining bright, in the night,
They wink and wave with delight.
A comet zooms, no visa in hand,
It's off to the next cosmic land.

Planets dance in a quirky show,
One's on a diet, the other's on dough.
Gravity's got jokes, it pulls at your soul,
While black holes just laugh, they swallow it whole.

Aliens laugh at our Earthly fears,
Trading their secrets over cold beers.
With space as a stage, we all play our parts,
In the vast universe, we share our hearts.

So let's raise our glasses, to cosmic cheer,
To light years of friendship, let's give a big leer.
Farewell to the worries, let's reach for the stars,
In this galaxy's circus, we're all shining czars.

Celestial Timekeepers

Tick-tock goes the cosmic clock,
Stars take selfies, it's quite a shock.
Planets scheduling lunch at noon,
While comets moonwalk to a funky tune.

Saturn wears rings, oh so stylish,
While Neptune's vibe is the most childish.
Mercury runs fast, it's on a spree,
While Jupiter's reading a cosmic decree.

Black holes are snooze buttons, oh so sly,
They swallow our plans, without a goodbye.
Yet time drips like honey, sweet and slow,
As we skip through the cosmos with a gleeful glow.

Watch the universe dance, with laughter and glee,
In a ticklish place where time's just a spree.
We're stardust timekeepers, filled with delight,
Laughing at the chaos of day and night.

A Symphony Across the Cosmos

Galaxies hum the most bizarre tunes,
While quasars twinkle like playful raccoons.
The Milky Way whispers secrets so deep,
While asteroids tumble with rhythmic beats.

Nebulas splatter colors on black, so bold,
While aliens gather for a dance of gold.
Jupiter strums on a giant guitar,
And Pluto's just chilling, a cosmic bazaar.

Shooting stars sprint, racing the sound,
With cosmic jokes in endless abound.
Every planet joins in this whimsical play,
Creating a symphony that brightens the way.

Oh, to be part of this vast cosmic choir,
Where laughter and music lift us higher.
Across the cosmos, let's sing and prance,
In this galactic gala, let's take a chance.

Reflections in a Darkened Infinity

In the void where echoes collide,
Reflections twist, with nowhere to hide.
A mirror ball spins, in a starry night,
With disco lights shining, a comical sight.

Asteroids giggle, we dance around,
As we float in silence, without a sound.
Nebulas twirl in a feathery gown,
While black holes snicker, wearing a frown.

Time bends and breaks, like a rubber band,
As we frolic through galaxies, hand in hand.
Wormholes whisper, 'Come play with us,'
While dark matter giggles, no need to discuss.

So let's spin together, in this playful jest,
With reflections of laughter, we'll never rest.
In this darkened infinity, let joy be our guide,
In the cosmic playground, let's take a wild ride.

Orbital Tranquility

Floating on my chair,
Coffee spills in zero-g,
Planets laugh below,
Astronauts dance for fun.

My sock slips from my foot,
Chasing it—what a great sprint!
It wraps around a star,
I guess it's lost for now.

Out here, fish fly past me,
With rocket fins and big smiles,
They wave their scaly tails,
Time for a fishy race!

Napping near a comet,
A pillow made of stardust,
Space dreams are their best,
Oh, I love cosmic naps!

Celestial Cartographer's Notes

Drawing maps in the dark,
Accidentally a doodle,
One big wiggly line,
Oops, that was a black hole!

Stars say they won't take calls,
They're busy having a blast,
Making new constellations,
What are they drawing now?

Comets flying by fast,
I wave, they wave back with tails,
It's a celestial dance,
How do they practice though?

Got lost on Mars last week,
Asked a sage cactus near,
He just laughed on his rock,
Was he joking or wise?

The Soft Glimmering Night

The moon's got a big grin,
Winking at the sleeping earth,
Stars chuckle in clusters,
What a merry night sky!

A satellite gets shy,
Blushing while it floats by,
Throwing out funny memes,
Witty in its own way.

Saturn's rings look like fries,
Had to take a quick bite,
Now I'm full of stardust,
Best snack I've ever had!

Jupiter's storms do sing,
Dancing clouds swirl around,
I think I'll join this waltz,
Two-step with gas giants!

Constellation Dreams

Drawing shapes in the sky,
I see a sandwich there,
Or was it a taco?
The Great Space Snack Parade!

Leo's tail's a long kite,
Floats during the cosmic breeze,
What if it gets tangled,
Will he need a space friend?

Stargazing, eyes tired,
Suddenly I'm a hero,
With capes made of starlight,
I save the day—again!

Planets play hide and seek,
Count to ten—where are they?
Nothing beats space fun,
When the cosmos join in!

Echoes of the Void

In the vast night sky,
Aliens drink martinis.
'Who ordered the stars?'
They laugh with glee.

Asteroids like bowling balls,
Strike them with a grin.
Galactic gutter balls
Make their heads spin.

Space whales hum a tune,
While spinning through the dust.
They misplace their keys
And sing, 'We must!'

Planets swap their names,
Jupiter cries, 'I'm Mars!'
Even black holes binge,
On candy bars!

Celestial Silhouettes

Stars wear silly hats,
Comets with long hair.
Moon dances like a pro,
In cosmic fair.

Neptune plays guitar,
Pluto joins the beat.
They throw a party,
For stardust to eat.

Saturn spins in style,
With rings that jingle.
Jovial giants cheer,
As space cats mingle.

Uranus cracks a joke,
And everyone laughs.
Galaxies collide,
In silly drafts!

Alien Reflections

In a spaceship zoom,
Aliens sip tea.
'What's the WiFi code?'
'Beep boop,' says he.

Earthlings wave hello,
With fingers and toes.
Aliens wave back,
With wiggly nose.

Spaceships run on cheese,
Fuel from the moon's crust.
They land on strange worlds,
Saying, 'You must!'

Saucers flip and flop,
As aliens play tag.
In zero gravity,
They giggle and brag.

Beyond the Event Horizon

Time slows down for laughs,
Inside the black void.
Gravitational pranks
Leave us overjoyed.

Spaghetti just bends,
As pasta in space.
'Why don't we stay here?'
Said the cosmic ace.

Wonky wormholes pop,
Swallowing our snacks.
And just for the fun,
They give them all back!

Dancing in the dark,
With comets that glide.
We twirl to the beat,
In this galactic ride!

Twilight Among the Stars

In the twilight glow,
Space squirrels gather nuts,
They've lost their acorns,
To a black hole's whim.

Zooming through the void,
Galactic frisbees fly,
Who needs gravity?
Let's just glide and laugh!

Cosmic coffee shops,
Served by Martian baristas,
With milk from Venus,
A funny, weird blend.

Stars wink and chuckle,
As planets spin their tales,
A universe full,
Of giggles and joy.

Shadows of Distant Suns

Dancing in the dark,
Alien shadows prance,
With no space for moves,
Just gliding mishaps.

Laughter from afar,
Echoes of supernova,
Too bright the punchline,
It burned out too soon!

Juggling asteroids,
One slips and cracks a smile,
A cosmic slapstick,
In the great beyond.

Suns wink at the stars,
Who trip on their starlit beams,
Gravity's not fair,
But giggles are shared.

Orbiting Memories

Round and round we go,
In a spiral of jokes,
Lost thoughts spinning fast,
In space's great buffet.

Floating past Pluto,
A ghostly cat chases light,
It thinks it's a star,
What a furry mess!

Toasters in orbit,
Making bread among the moons,
A cosmic breakfast,
Sliced with giggles bright.

Forgotten moments,
Drift like lost satellites,
We laugh at the void,
As we orbit joy.

Pulsar's Heartbeat

A pulsar's rhythm,
Keeps time with cosmic beats,
Little stars dance by,
To their own weird tunes.

Space-time jokes abound,
Light years flow in laughter,
Wormholes twist and shout,
What a dizzy ride!

Galaxies collide,
In a game of tag and chase,
Stars tickle each other,
With comets on the side.

Eternal giggles,
Echo through the dark vastness,
In this cosmic joke,
We all play our part.

Nebular Whirlwinds

Galaxies spin round,
Stars get dizzy, fall down.
Planets play hide-and-seek,
Catch them if you are meek.

Asteroids dance near,
Twirl and shake with no fear.
Comets with silly tails,
Laugh as they leave trails.

Aliens on a spree,
Running wild, full of glee.
They just missed the start,
Of a very long mart.

Across the vast space,
Rockets flip with much grace.
In zero-G they roll,
Space is one funny stroll.

Threads of Cosmic Light

Cosmic fibers weave,
Wormholes make us believe.
Light bulbs from the stars,
Swap jokes from afar.

Quasars chuckle bright,
Pulsing with cosmic light.
Neutrinos play cards,
Laughing at home yards.

Black holes, what a sight!
Swallowing all in bite.
But they'll burp with glee,
Spitting stars over the sea.

Eclipses wear shades,
As they dance in parades.
Sun and moon, best friends,
Playing until day ends.

Celestial Constellations in Bloom

Stars bloom like flowers,
In the dark, they bring hours.
A dandelion star,
Wishes upon a car.

Orion takes a bow,
With a proud cosmic wow.
Pleiades giggle bright,
Twinkling through the night.

Ursa's bear jokes loud,
Laughing with the whole crowd.
Spilling some sweet tea,
Underneath the old tree.

Venus throws a fit,
In the sky, loves to sit.
While Mars tries to dance,
But stumbles in a trance.

Phenomena of the Infinite Sky

Rainbows in the void,
Supernovae deployed.
Dancing with delight,
In the starry night.

Waves crash in the dark,
Galactic dreams embark.
Black holes rumble fun,
Swallowing everyone.

Cosmic jokes go round,
Echoing without sound.
Planets trip and fall,
As they play bounce-ball.

Space-time's silly loop,
Time runs in a group.
Relativity laughs,
While we draw our graphs.

Fragments of Starlight

Shining on my cheese,
A comet flies by fast,
I grab my telescope,
For cosmic grilled delight.

Asteroids make a mess,
In my cosmic picnic,
Planets roll like marbles,
Space games got out of hand!

Shooting stars do the splits,
Wishing well's running low,
Aliens sell real estate,
In a galaxy far, far out!

Neutron stars play catch,
Quasars laugh out loud,
Black holes pull my snacks in,
Taste-test at light speed!

Celestial Bloom

Roses grow on Mars,
Petals shaped like stars,
Gardening on moons,
Using space shovels too!

Saturn's rings are bling,
Dressed for a dance party,
Planets take a spin,
Wobbling to space beats!

Cosmic bees buzz loud,
Pollinating stardust,
Honey from black holes,
Sweetness of the void!

Lunar lettuce jumps,
Bouncing in low gravity,
Salad dreams take flight,
Dinner in the stars!

Dance of the Galaxies

Galaxies twirl around,
Spinning on a whim,
Wormholes play DJ,
With beats that warp the time!

Stars wear funky hats,
Shooting disco lights,
Pulsars make a scene,
In a cosmic dance-off!

Space oddities slide,
Gravity's not a rule,
Dances defy logic,
As comets waltz like pros!

Space-time's punchy tune,
Drifting through the void,
Supernovas pop,
Groovy in the night!

Aetherial Haunts

Ghosts of comets laugh,
Spooking the starry skies,
They peek through craters,
Making planets jumpy!

Whimsical whistlers,
Sing tunes on moonlit nights,
Saturn's shy phantoms,
Dance under starry veils.

Aliens tell tales,
Of mischief in the void,
Floating through stardust,
Trading spooky secrets!

Black holes tell bad jokes,
Pulling laughter with ease,
In the cosmic gloom,
Spookiness prevails!

Dreaming in Cosmic Dust

Stars are winking bright,
I trip on moonbeams,
Space squirrels chat away,
Their jokes are quite the meme.

Galaxies in a spin,
Do they ever get dizzy?
Floating in their own gin,
Oh, that sounds quite fizzy!

Planets wear silly hats,
Dance like no one's watching,
Comets play tag with bats,
In space, it's all quite thrilling!

Black holes make a grand call,
"Jump in! The view is grand!"
Will I float or just fall?
Oh well, just take my hand!

Constellations of Thought

Whispers in the sky,
Orion sings out loud,
His belt's gone awry,
"Who dressed me in this crowd?"

Venus in her prime,
Dances with Mars so bold,
She says, "I'm just in time!"
He replies, "Don't be cold!"

Pleiades are quite shy,
They giggle in the night,
"Did you see that guy?
He just winked; what a sight!"

Star clusters throw a bash,
Cosmic karaoke fun,
Singing 'til the crash,
A galactic midnight run!

Celestial Ballet

The sun takes center stage,
With flair, he winks and bows,
While planets turn the page,
And dance like disco cows.

Asteroids in the back,
They're not quite on the beat,
Stumbling in their track,
But still they feel the heat!

Nebulas spin in twirls,
Sprinkling dust like glitter,
"Look at us, we're girls!
Shiny, not just a flitter!"

Uranus gives a spin,
"Oh dear, what a surprise!"
"Who let the dogs begin?"
A planet's fun in disguise!

Rhapsody of Celestial Bodies

Moons waltz in a line,
Twisting with all their might,
"Hey, do you see that sign?
'No dancing after night!'"

Jupiter's a DJ,
Spinning tracks of slow jams,
While Saturn takes a break,
Wearing sparkly slam bands.

It's a party on Mars,
They've got snacks made of dust,
"Try the cheese from afar!
It's the best, trust me, just!"

In the dark of space wide,
Shooting stars glide with grace,
"Just make a wish," they cried,
"And maybe win this race!"

Astral Tides

Waves of light we ride,
Cosmic surfboards gliding wide.
Stars chuckle as we drift,
Making the galaxies shift.

Aliens with ice cream,
Pouring stardust in their dream.
Planets spinning on a spree,
Who knew space could be so free?

Meteor showers rain,
Umbrellas? Not in this domain!
We dodge with style and grace,
While comets laugh at our race.

In this cosmic ballet,
Giggles echo night and day.
Dance with me on moonbeam trails,
Where laughter never fails.

Echoes of Distant Worlds

In a far-off galaxy,
Aliens throw a raucous tea.
They sip on cosmic brew,
While parsing human's latest view.

Planets party, music blares,
Saturn shows off, and how it flares!
Jupiter steals the show,
Does a dance, puts on a glow.

"Earthlings, join our fun!" they shout,
With space snacks, there's no doubt.
We learn to groove and sway,
While stars wink and spin away.

Echoes ripple through the night,
As laughter takes its flight.
In this cosmic jam we sing,
With joy that space will always bring.

Solar Winds and Stardust

Solar winds that tickle toes,
Stardust played a game of shows.
Whirling on a cosmic slide,
Sunbeams bursting, can't hide!

Riding rays with silly grins,
We outrun time; let's begin!
Photons play tag, speeding bright,
While black holes wait to bite.

A disco ball, the sun does spin,
Glistening hues we take it in.
With laughter ringing clear,
As planets join the cheer.

Galactic winds blow, what a rush,
In this funny cosmic hush.
Embrace the whims of space today,
Where joy and laughter find their way.

The Dance of Celestial Bodies

Galaxies do the twist,
Stars shine, they can't resist.
Gravity pulls us in a whirl,
Comets dive and softly twirl.

Orbiting around with flair,
Dancing partners, do they care?
Moon beeps, "Join my waltz, oh please!"
In the sky, we laugh with ease.

Asteroids clapping, quite the show,
Planets take a turn, then go.
In this cosmic dance we spin,
With giggles floating on the wind.

So come, my friend, let's frolic free,
In this ballet of galaxy!
Where every star has a chance to play,
With humor brightens up the way.

Infinity Between Stars

Stars poke fun at us,
Light years dance in puns.
Space asks, 'Where's your ship?'
We laugh in cosmic runs.

Galaxies roll their eyes,
Comets chuckle bright.
Stardust is the confetti,
In this vast delight.

Planets spin in circles,
Suns wink with glee.
Black holes play hide and seek,
What a sight to see!

Time is just a prankster,
Rolling in a ball.
Flying through the vibrant void,
We're laughing after all.

Voyage of the Comet's Tail

A comet zooms by,
Waving its long hair,
Stars poke fun at it,
'Hey! Don't you get care?'

Zipping through the night,
Sparkles trailing low,
It giggles at dark moons,
Where the space cats glow.

Asteroids play catch,
With a wink and a spin,
While aliens sip tea,
In their faraway din.

It's a merry chase,
Amongst cosmic haze,
The tail leaves a spark,
In this funny maze.

Light Years of Silence

In the quiet of night,
Stars whisper and tease,
'You're light years from me,
But buddy, just breathe.'

Nebulas make faces,
With colors so bold,
They laugh at our worries,
'You're never too old!'

Planets trot around,
In their fancy shoes,
Jupiter spins jokes,
With his joyful blues.

While black holes giggle,
Sucking stars like sweets,
Laughter echoes wide,
In these stellar heats.

The Void's Gentle Touch

The void gives a pat,
'Just relax, don't fret.'
While shooting stars play tag,
In a cosmic net.

Constellations grinning,
Forming silly shapes,
With a wink and nudge,
Creating funny tapes.

Astro-bunnies bounce,
In the weightless air,
They hop past from stars,
With a giggle flare.

In the depths of space,
Joyful silence reigns,
Whispers of the void,
Amidst laughter's chains.

Planetary Perspectives

Mars wears a little hat,
Jupiter laughs with gas,
Venus is stuck in traffic,
While Earth plays catch with grass.

Saturn spins ribbons of light,
Uranus winks with a sigh,
Neptune's lost some of its blue,
As Pluto rolls his eye.

Mercury races too fast,
Sun says, "Slow down my friend!"
But Mercury just speeds up,
Chasing light 'til the end.

There's a comet in a tutu,
Waltzing through the dark night sky,
While the moons all giggle softly,
Making wishes as they fly.

The Sound of Stars Colliding

Two stars bumped, oh my gosh!
What a spark, what a noise!
They meant to dance quite softly,
But lost their graceful poise.

Supernova giggles loud,
As black holes spin and swirl,
Gravity's great at hugs,
But sometimes it makes you twirl.

A meteorite whispers jokes,
To asteroids passing by,
They chuckle in the silence,
Until one asks, "Why'd I fly?"

Galaxies chat over tea,
In a spiral of delight,
They discuss the just-found planets,
As they twinkle through the night.

Astrological Reverence

Saturn's rings dance for cheer,
While Pisces swims in place.
Virgo counts the stars with care,
And Libra finds the grace.

Scorpio stings with laughter,
As Gemini plays a tune,
Aries jumps, and Taurus eats,
Beneath the watchful moon.

Capricorn drinks stardust tea,
Leo strikes a pose,
Aquarius shares wild dreams,
While Cancer ebbs and flows.

These signs meet in the cosmos,
To share cosmic memes,
Planets roll their eyes above,
Fruit loops float in streams.

The Melodies of Orbits

In a whirl of cosmic sound,
Orbits play their sweet refrain,
The sun hums low and mellow,
Planets join in, sing the same.

Mercury taps with quick little beats,
While Venus hums a note so pure,
Earth adds claps, a rhythm divine,
And Mars shakes its dust for sure.

Jupiter's bass rumbles deep,
Saturn twirls like a disco light,
Uranus brings a funky flair,
As Neptune winks, all is bright.

In this galactic jamboree,
Stars are the dazzling choir,
Together they sing the night away,
Lighting up our cosmic fire.

Cosmic Cradles

Stars are cradles bright,
Naptime in zero-G,
Floating past moons that shout,
"Wake me for lunch, please!"

Asteroids make great beds,
Pillow fights with comets,
Galaxies spin and giggle,
While aliens toss donuts.

Milky Way's a buffet,
Cosmic treats on display,
Planets play ring toss games,
Laughing in their own way.

Liftoff from grumpy Earth,
Space cats chase laser beams,
Slingshot around the sun,
Just to hear some space screams.

Orbiting Reveries

Planets dance a waltz,
Twinkling in pure delight,
Saturn spins in style,
With rings that shine so bright.

Comet tails like kites,
Glide through the vast unknown,
Astro-nuts throw parties,
While gravity's overthrown.

Jupiter's a jukebox,
Playing tunes that resonate,
It's hard not to boogie,
When you're orbiting fate.

Nebulae are hosts,
For galactic potlucks,
E.T. cooks spaghetti,
While we share some starstruck.

Forgotten Celestial Fables

Once there was a star,
Who dreamed of being gold,
But turned out to be gas,
Now tells tales, bold and old.

Black holes with jokes galore,
Swallow laughter whole,
While wormholes play hide and seek,
Hoping to catch a soul.

Sunflowers bloom on Mars,
Singing in cosmic waves,
They share poetic tales,
From alien cave raves.

Titan's shy, but funny,
Waves splash in muted hues,
A trove of silly stories,
That outer space renews.

Among the Stars' Whispers

Stars gossip at twilight,
Swapping tales of love's plight,
Whirling with stardust giggles,
In the soft velvet night.

Asteroids chirp and chime,
With melodies so sweet,
They jive around the sun,
As if dancing on their feet.

Folklore of cosmic friends,
Shared beneath moonlit skies,
They chuckle and they smile,
As the universe flies.

In the realm of wonder,
Laughter fills the vast space,
Eternal cosmic joy,
In this funny, wild place.

Celestial Homecoming

Flying through the stars, so bright,
Left my keys on a comet's flight.
Home's a bit far, I must admit,
But the view is nice, and I won't quit.

Space snacks floating, what a treat!
I'll enjoy this cosmic seat.
Gravity, where did you go?
Do I float, or just take it slow?

Getting lost in cosmic maps,
Feeling silly in starry traps.
Navigating by my gut,
Oops! Just hit that solar hut.

Finally, home, the place I seek,
Forgot my wallet—oh, how meek!
But laughter echoes in the void,
Galactic giggles have not cloyed.

Lost in a Celestial Labyrinth

Stuck in space, round and round,
Where's the exit? No clue found.
Navigating through the stars,
Who thought this would be so bizarre?

Dust bunny planets start to tease,
Floating on a cosmic breeze.
Caught in webs of starlight strands,
Do I follow or make demands?

Aliens laugh at my lost face,
"Join us for a dance in space!"
I trip over a moonlit beam,
What a joke, this cosmic dream!

"Left or right?" I call in vain,
Stars reply with silent gain.
Chasing shadows of my snacks,
Life in space is full of whacks!

Spheres of Influence

Caught between two moons so wide,
One wants to hug, the other, glide.
"Come here," says one, "No, stay away!"
Spheres of influence in dismay.

Gravity's a fickle friend,
Pulling me to where it'll end.
Floating free, I spin and sway,
In this cosmic ballet, hooray!

"Are you my moon?" I joke and grin,
"Not unless we can both fit in!"
They laugh and roll in space-time whirl,
Cosmos jokes for every twirl.

To dance with stars and call them kin,
What a wild ride, let's begin!
In this sphere of endless play,
Let's orbit laughter every day!

Cosmic Threads Unraveled

Knots of stars I try to tease,
Like misdirected cosmic cheese.
Trying to braid a comet's tail,
With laughter echoing in the gale.

Shooting stars form silly lines,
Dancing through galactic vines.
"Oops, stitched a black hole by mistake!"
"I'll fix it later; give me a break!"

Galaxies giggle, twinkling bright,
Threading humor into the night.
Cosmic yarn gets tangled, oh dear,
But unraveling brings out cheer!

At the end, it's all a show,
Tangled laughter in the flow.
Space threads connect us, that's the deal,
In this cosmic dance, we all feel!

www.ingramcontent.com/pod-product-compliance
Lightning Source LLC
Chambersburg PA
CBHW071841160426
43209CB00003B/376